NORRIE EXPLORES...

SHANGHAI

Help Norrie to solve the clues on a fascinating adventure!

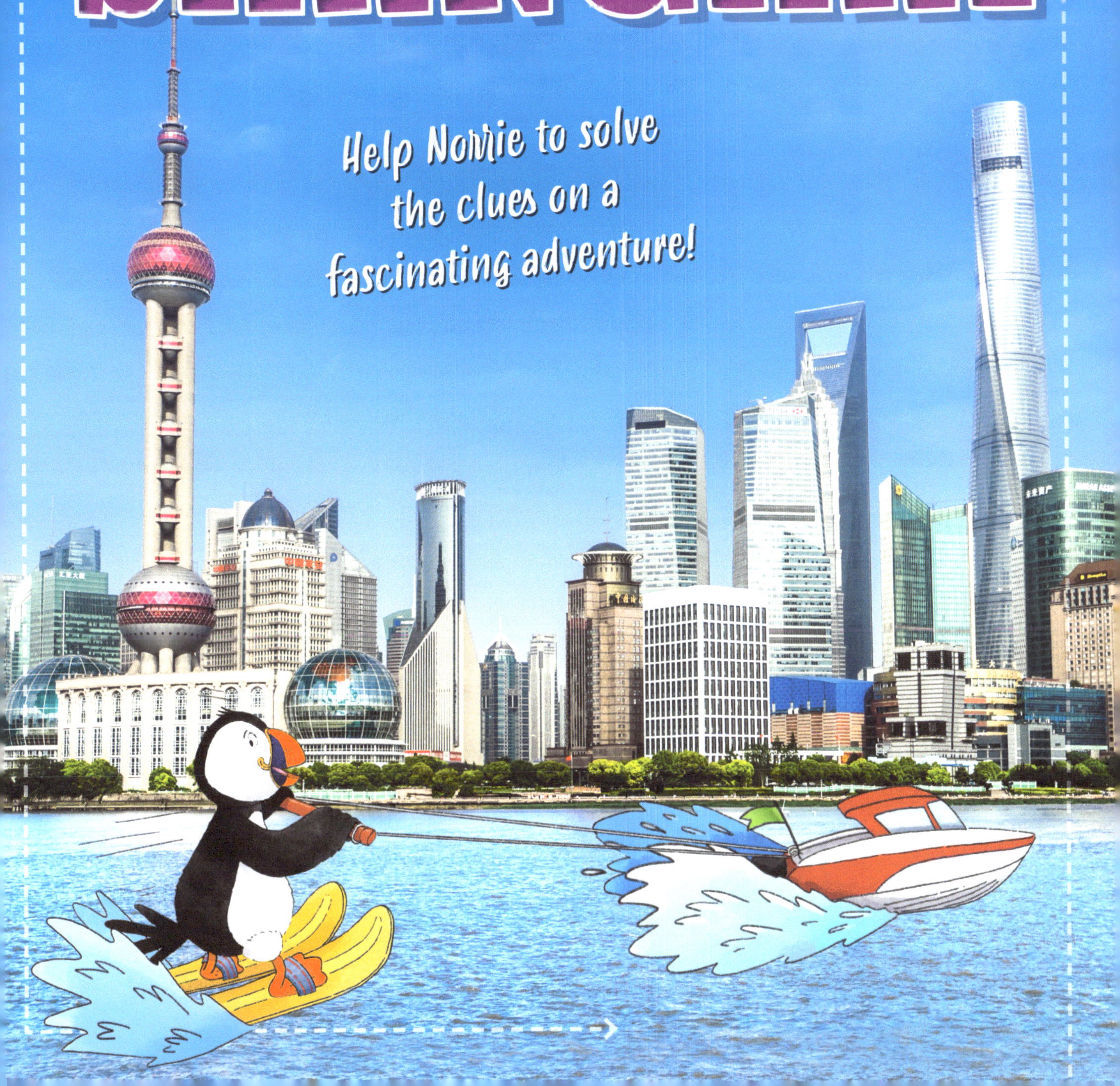

World Book, Inc.
180 North LaSalle Street
Suite 900
Chicago, Illinois 60601
USA

For information about other World Book publications, visit our website at www.worldbook.com or call 1-800-WORLDBK (967-5325). For information about sales to schools and libraries, call 1-800-975-3250 (United States), or 1-800-837-5365 (Canada).

Library of Congress Cataloging-in-Publication Data for this volume has been applied for.

Norrie Explores ...
ISBN: 978-0-7166-5303-5 (set, hc.)

Norrie Explores ... Shanghai
ISBN: 978-0-7166-5311-0 (hc.)
ISBN: 978-0-7166-5331-8 (pf.)

Also available as:
ISBN: 978-0-7166-5321-9 (e-book)

Staff

Acknowledgments

Writer: Izzi Howell
Illustrator: Lizzie Walkley

Developed with World Book by
White-Thomson Publishing LTD
www.wtpub.co.uk

Cover: Norrie artwork by Lizzie Walkley, Advocate Art; © Chunyip Wong, iStock

4-5 © Chunyip Wong, iStock
6-7 © Mark Andrews, Alamy Images; © Markus Mainka, Shutterstock
8-9 © Beauty Studio/Shutterstock; © Gionnixxx/iStock
10-11 © Cho Minjun, Shutterstock; © Jon Arnold Images/Alamy Images
12-13 © Stockinasia/iStock; © Mauritius images GmbH/Alamy Images
14-15 © Peter Horree, Alamy Images; © Efired/Shutterstock
16-17 © Songquan Deng, Alamy Images; © Michael DeFreitas Asia/Alamy Images; © Mariano Garcia, Alamy Images
18-19 © Incamerastock/Alamy Images; © 4045/Shutterstock
20-21 © Shutterstock
22-23 © Daizuoxin/iStock; © Imaginechina Limited/Alamy Images
24-25 © Ian Dagnall, Alamy Images; © Sergi Reboredo, Alamy Images
26-27 © Kevin Ma, Alamy Images; © George Brice, Alamy Images
28-29 © cyoginan/iStock; © Design Pics Inc/Alamy Images
30-31 © Yuen Man Cheung, Alamy Images; © Yongyuan Dai, iStock
32-33 © Xinhua/Alamy Images; © Chris Stock Photography/Alamy Images
34-35 © Iain Masterton, Alamy Images; © Weiming Xie, Shutterstock; © Ivar Skoglund, Shutterstock; © Stayang/Shutterstock
36-37 © Llewellyn/Alamy Images; © Avalon/Construction Photography/Alamy Images
38-39 © Alex-VN/Alamy Images; © Alexander Kondakov, Alamy Images
40-41 © Clickalps SRLs/SuperStock; © Tatiana Popova, Shutterstock
42-43 © Qin Xie, Alamy Images; © Ronnie Chua, Alamy Images; © Kungfu01/Shutterstock; © Prasit Rodphan, Alamy Images
46-47 © Imaginechina Limited/Alamy Images; © Shutterstock
48-49 © Shutterstock; SSYoung (licensed under CC BY-SA 4.0)
50-51 © Shutterstock

Contents

Welcome to Shanghai!

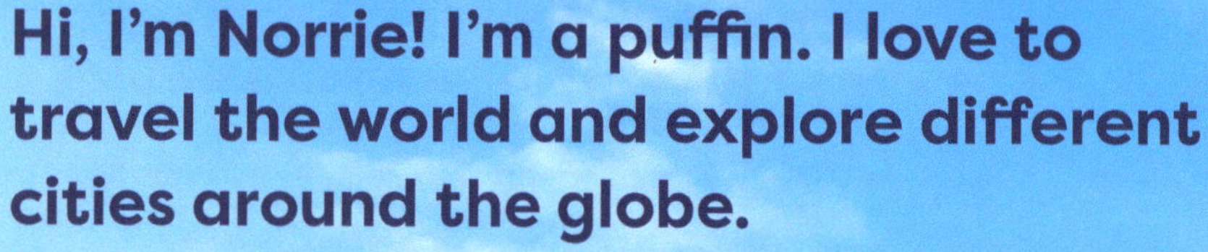

Hi, I'm Norrie! I'm a puffin. I love to travel the world and explore different cities around the globe.

Today, I'm in Shanghai, the largest city in China. China is a country on the continent of Asia. Have you ever visited Shanghai or China before?

Up until the middle of the 1800's, Shanghai was a small trading town. That all changed in 1842 when the city was opened up to trade with other countries. People from France, the United Kingdom, the United States, and other countries settled in Shanghai in special areas for foreigners. Shanghai became a world leader in trading and banking. Today, the city is an important center of industry, trade, and finance and is home to around 22,500,000 people.

Look at those skyscrapers! I can't wait to explore!

Last week, I received a mysterious letter inviting me to Shanghai. I have no idea who sent it or why! The letter told me to look out for clues around the city that would lead me to a secret location. I love solving puzzles, so I'm really excited to see where the clues will take me ... and explore the incredible city of Shanghai, of course! Will you help me solve the clues and find my way around Shanghai?

Shanghai lies on the banks of the Huangpu River in the eastern part of China.

Maglev trains

My plane landed at Shanghai Pudong International Airport, and now I need to travel into the city center. The best way to get there is by maglev train.

Maglev stands for magnetic levitation. These trains use magnetic force to float above the tracks. This means that they can move much faster than normal trains because there is no friction between the train and the track. In fact, the Shanghai maglev trains are the world's fastest commercial trains! It takes them no more than 8 minutes to travel the 19 miles (31 kilometers) between the airport and Longyang Road station.

The Shanghai maglev trains have been carrying passengers to and from the airport since 2003.

Whoa! That ride was so quick. Here at Longyang Road station, there's a museum where you can learn more about maglev trains and how they work. There are maglev trains in other countries around the world, too, such as Japan and South Korea.

The Shanghai maglev trains are the fastest, though, so I'm glad I got the chance to ride on one. Longyang Road station connects to the Shanghai Metro system, which will take me into downtown Shanghai.

Wukang Road

Don't worry ... we're still in China! But in the past, some parts of Shanghai, known as concessions, were ruled over and settled by people from other countries.

This road here, which is now known as Wukang Road, was part of the French concession from 1849 to 1946.

So how did this all start? Well, in 1842, the United Kingdom won a war against China and forced the country to open Shanghai to foreign trade. The United Kingdom set up a concession here in the city, followed by France, the United States, and Japan. These settlements ended around the time of World War II (1939-1945).

The Wukang Mansion is one of the most famous buildings on the Wukang Road. It used to be split into different apartments. Many Chinese movie stars lived here in the 1930's and 1940's.

The settlers constructed many different styles of buildings in each concession, inspired by different types of architecture from around the world. Here on Wukang Road, there are many large mansions. Some look French, others look British, and some have an Art Deco style. Art Deco was a popular style of design in the 1920's and 1930's.

Xintiandi

Xintiandi is a modern pedestrian shopping area ... with a history!

Many of the buildings here have been converted from traditional Shanghainese houses, known as shikumen. These historical homes are now luxury stores, restaurants, and cafes. It's a wonderful place to explore and learn more about the history of this city!

Shikumen houses are tall brick townhouses built around a narrow alleyway. The alleyway was connected to the main road through a stone archway. Each shikumen house had a courtyard, hidden behind a tall brick wall. Shikumen houses combined features of Western and Chinese architecture. Terraced townhouses were common in Western cities, while Chinese houses often had courtyards.

Shikumen houses were built in Shanghai for about 100 years, from the mid-1800's onwards. In the 1930's, 60 percent of the houses in Shanghai were shikumen style. Now, only a few remain. Most homes in the center of Shanghai are now modern apartment blocks. What type of home do you live in?

Jing'an Temple

Jing'an Temple is one of the most famous places of worship in Shanghai. This Buddhist temple is tucked away between tall modern buildings and busy roads.

Buddhism has been an important religion in China throughout the country's history. Today, it is one of the five religions recognized by the Chinese government, along with Taoism, Islam, Protestantism, and Catholicism.

The first version of Jing'an Temple was built all the way back in A.D. 247! It was moved to this location nearly one thousand years later, in 1216. Today, over 800 years on, the temple still stands in the same spot, although the buildings themselves have been destroyed and rebuilt many times over the years.

Time to take a look inside the temple. There's so much to look at! Inside the Mahavira Hall is the largest jade Buddha in China. It stands at 12.4 feet (3.8 meters) tall and weighs an incredible 12 tons (11 tons). The statue is so large that one wall of the hall had to be removed to get it in! There's also an old copper bell that dates from the Ming Dynasty (1368 to 1644).

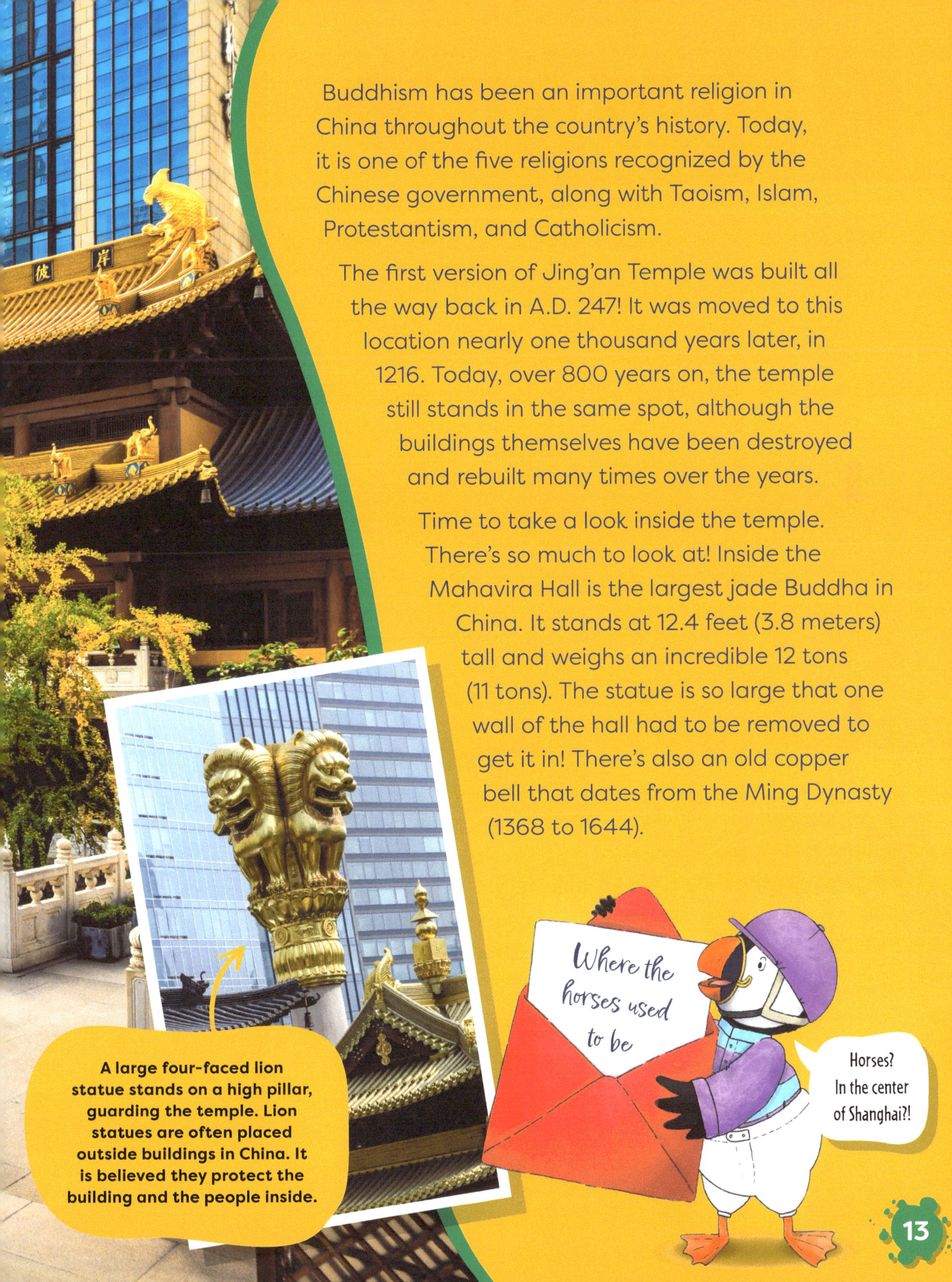

A large four-faced lion statue stands on a high pillar, guarding the temple. Lion statues are often placed outside buildings in China. It is believed they protect the building and the people inside.

People's Square

It's hard to tell today, but this huge square used to be the site of a British racetrack!

In the 1950's, the site was turned into a large park, called the People's Park, and the massive People's Square, which is where I am now! The People's Square is Shanghai's largest public open space.

Many important buildings and museums are built around the square. Let's explore! That tall, squared building is the Shanghai People's Government building, the headquarters of Shanghai's municipal government. Then there's the Shanghai Grand Theater, which is home to the Shanghai Opera House. Here, you can watch Chinese and international operas, concerts, ballet performances, and much more.

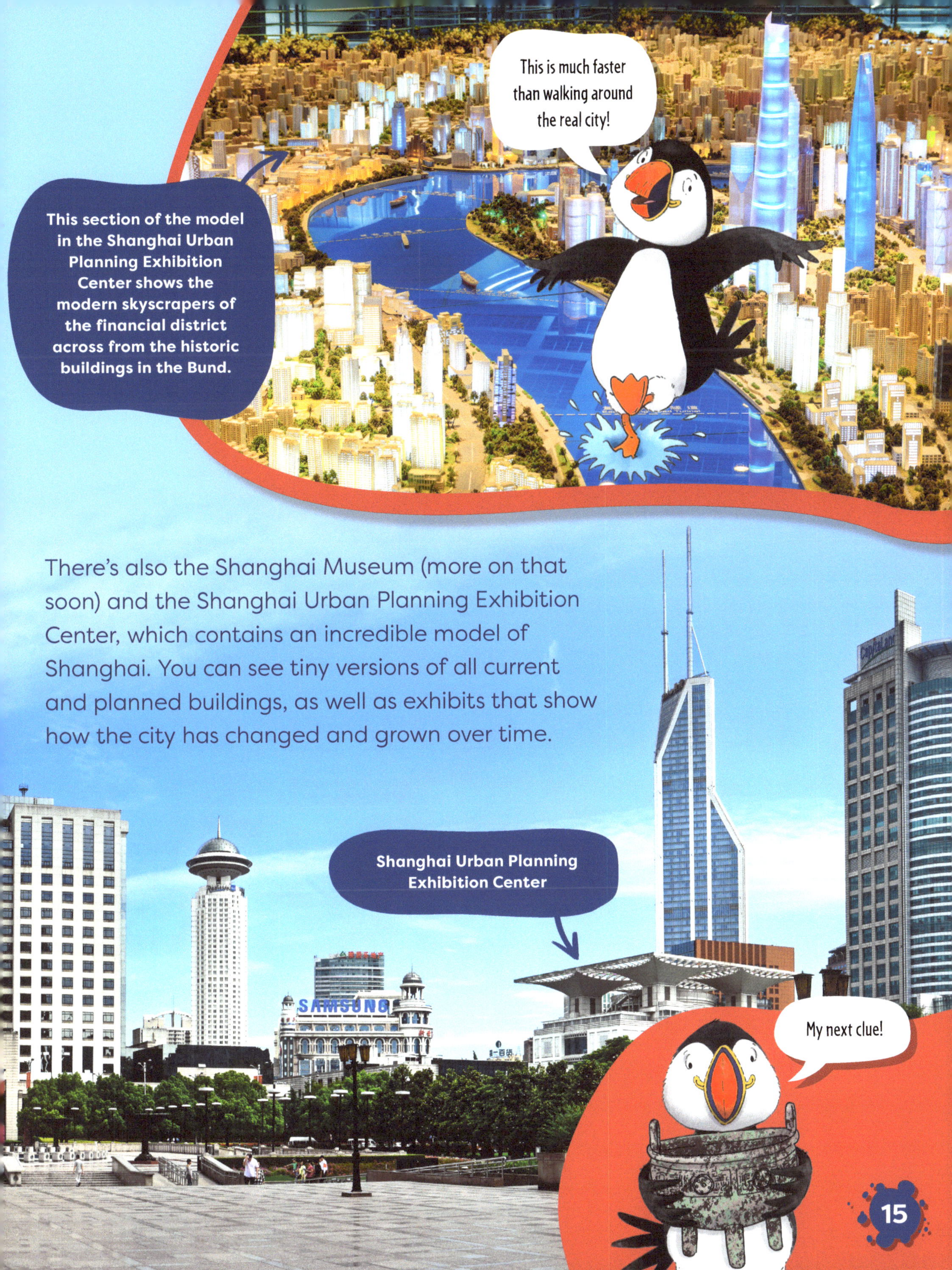

There's also the Shanghai Museum (more on that soon) and the Shanghai Urban Planning Exhibition Center, which contains an incredible model of Shanghai. You can see tiny versions of all current and planned buildings, as well as exhibits that show how the city has changed and grown over time.

Shanghai Museum

Do you know what a ding is? Don't worry if you don't! (Look back at my last clue for a hint!) A ding is an ancient Chinese pot with legs.

Not only can you see some examples of dings here at the Shanghai Museum, but the shape of the building itself was also inspired by a ding! History inside and out ... that's my kind of museum!

The Shanghai Museum was founded in 1952. It was based in several smaller buildings. In 1996, it opened in this new building on the People's Square. Here, there is much more space for the museum's massive collection.

Oh yes, I can see it!

The shape of the Shanghai Museum, with its round top and square base, also reflects the ancient Chinese idea that the sky is round and Earth is square.

It contains over 120,000 pieces of ancient Chinese art, including paintings, bronzes, masks, sculptures, ceramics, jade carvings, furniture, coins, ... and dings of course! What shall I look at first?

Bronze dings, like this one, were used during religious rituals in the past. Ceramic dings were used for cooking and serving food.

Nanjing Road

I know! Running east from People's Square is one part of Nanjing Road – one of the busiest shopping streets in the world!

Around 1 million people visit every day. It's the perfect place to shop for souvenirs. You can find almost anything here – electronics, clothes, housewares, toiletries, and much more. The road is also traffic free, so you can stroll and window shop without checking for cars.

Nanjing Road is home to some of the largest and oldest department stores in Shanghai. They've been here since the early 1900's.

That's over one hundred of years of shopping! I wonder what the street looked like back then.

My legs are starting to ache after all that shopping! I'm going to hop on the Dangdang sightseeing tram to travel the rest of the way. It moves slowly so that people riding on the tram can take photos.

If you aren't as tired as me, you can explore the other part of Nanjing Road, which runs west from People's Square. This section of the road has many historic hotels and luxury shopping centers.

The Bund

This waterfront historical area is known as the Bund. It stretches for about one mile (1.6 kilometers) along the western side of the Huangpu River.

In the second half of the 1800's, the Bund was home to many banks, trading centers, and customs houses built by the people living in Shanghai's foreign concessions. This is why the buildings here have a traditional Western style of architecture. Today, some of these buildings are still used for trading and finance. Others are fancy hotels, offices, and luxury stores.

It's the perfect day to explore this riverside area. Across the river are many modern skyscrapers. I hope I get a chance to visit them later!

This building with the clock looks interesting. It's called the Custom House. There have been several customs houses on this site over the years, but this one was built in 1927. At the time, it was the tallest building on the Bund! Right next door is the HSBC Building. It's famous for its grand design with massive columns and a domed ceiling. The inside of the building is also luxurious. It is decorated with marble and mosaics (pictures made out of tiny tiles).

Right across the river

What's the best way across a river?

Bridges

The Huangpu River cuts through the center of Shanghai, and there are many more small rivers and creeks throughout the city. Luckily, there are plenty of bridges to help people and vehicles get around!

Waibaidu Bridge is one of the most famous bridges in the city. It's located next to the Bund. The first wooden bridge was built here in 1856. Before that, people had to get the ferry across! Since then, the bridge has been replaced three more times. The steel bridge standing today was built in 1907. Recently, LED lights were added to the bridge so that it can glow different colors at night! I'll have to come back later and see it for myself.

The Waibaidu Bridge is an example of a truss bridge. The structure above the bridge helps to distribute and support the weight of the bridge below.

Fun fact! The Yangpu Bridge was originally unpainted. It was painted red in 2000 to celebrate the millennium.

If you like bridges, don't forget to check out Yangpu Bridge, which crosses the Huangpu River. At 27,400 feet (8,354 meters) long, it's one of the longest bridges in the world! The bridge's cables support the weight of the deck below. However, the Yangpu Bridge is no match for the Donghai Bridge when it comes to length! This 20-mile (32.5-kilometer) bridge connects Shanghai to a deep-water port in the South China Sea. It's one of the longest cross-sea bridges in the world.

City God Temple

The City God Temple in Shanghai dates from 1403, making it over 600 years old! This temple is also known as the Chenghuang Temple.

In Chinese folk religion, a Chenghuang is a god who protects a city and all the people who live in it. The temple here is dedicated to Shanghai's three city gods.

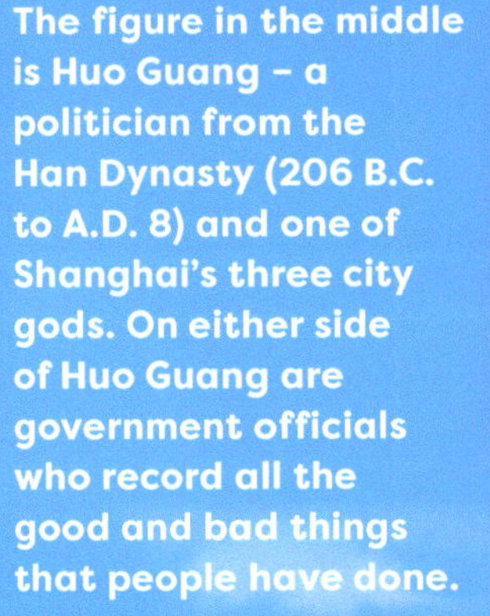

The figure in the middle is Huo Guang – a politician from the Han Dynasty (206 B.C. to A.D. 8) and one of Shanghai's three city gods. On either side of Huo Guang are government officials who record all the good and bad things that people have done.

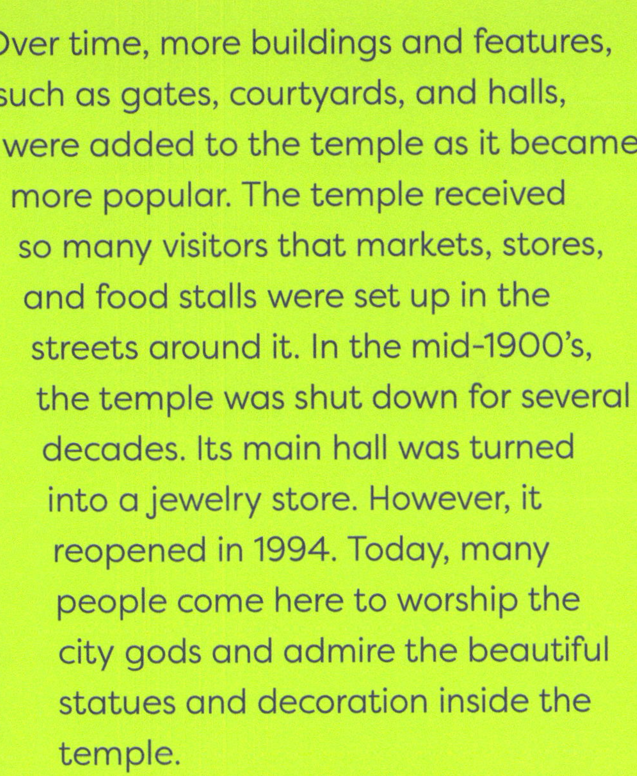

Over time, more buildings and features, such as gates, courtyards, and halls, were added to the temple as it became more popular. The temple received so many visitors that markets, stores, and food stalls were set up in the streets around it. In the mid-1900's, the temple was shut down for several decades. Its main hall was turned into a jewelry store. However, it reopened in 1994. Today, many people come here to worship the city gods and admire the beautiful statues and decoration inside the temple.

Yu Garden

Of course! The beautiful Yu Garden is a short walk from the City God Temple. It is just the place to sit and rest for a while.

The garden was first built over 400 years ago. Back then it was a private garden for an important politician and his family. Over the years, the garden has been damaged and rebuilt many times.

There is so much to explore in the garden's six different areas. I've spotted pools filled with bright orange fish, traditional Chinese pagodas (tiered towers), shady pavilions, and scenic bridges and walkways. Tall white walls decorated with a carved dragon's head surround each section. I wonder if I can spot all of the dragons on my walk around the garden!

I've heard that there is a very special bridge with nine turns in it here in the Yu Garden. It looks a bit like a zig-zag! Nine is a lucky number in China, so walking across the bridge is supposed to bring good luck. The bridge also leads to a teahouse. I'd love a cup of tea ... what good luck to have ended up here!

The Yu Garden is home to possibly the most famous stone in Shanghai – the Exquisite Jade Rock. This massive rock is made of soft limestone, which is easily worn away by water. This gives the rock its unusual shape.
I've got it!
A megatall tower

Shanghai Tower

All skyscrapers are tall, but the name "megatall" is reserved for the very highest buildings that reach 1,969 feet (600 meters) or more.

The Shanghai Tower is located in Lujiazui – the financial center of Shanghai. There are many skyscrapers here, such as the Jin Mao Tower and the Shanghai World Financial Center.

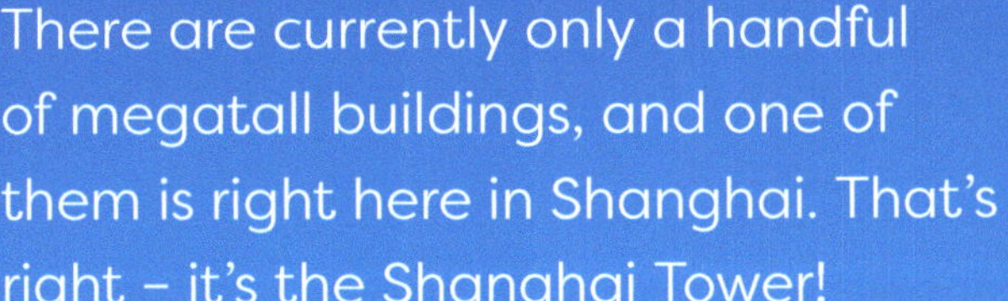

There are currently only a handful of megatall buildings, and one of them is right here in Shanghai. That's right – it's the Shanghai Tower!

This massive skyscraper is an incredible 2,073 feet (632 meters) tall. This makes it the tallest building in China and the third tallest building in the world. Unsurprisingly for such a tall structure, it also has the highest observation deck of any building. There, you can look down over the city from a dizzying height of 1,844 feet (562 meters).

But don't worry if heights aren't your thing. The Shanghai Tower has so much more to entertain visitors, including restaurants, stores, a spa, and a swimming pool. There are also hotels and offices.

Eeek! It's a long way down! But now that I see the other skyscrapers from up here at the top of the Shanghai Tower, I understand just how tall it really is!

I recognize that tower!

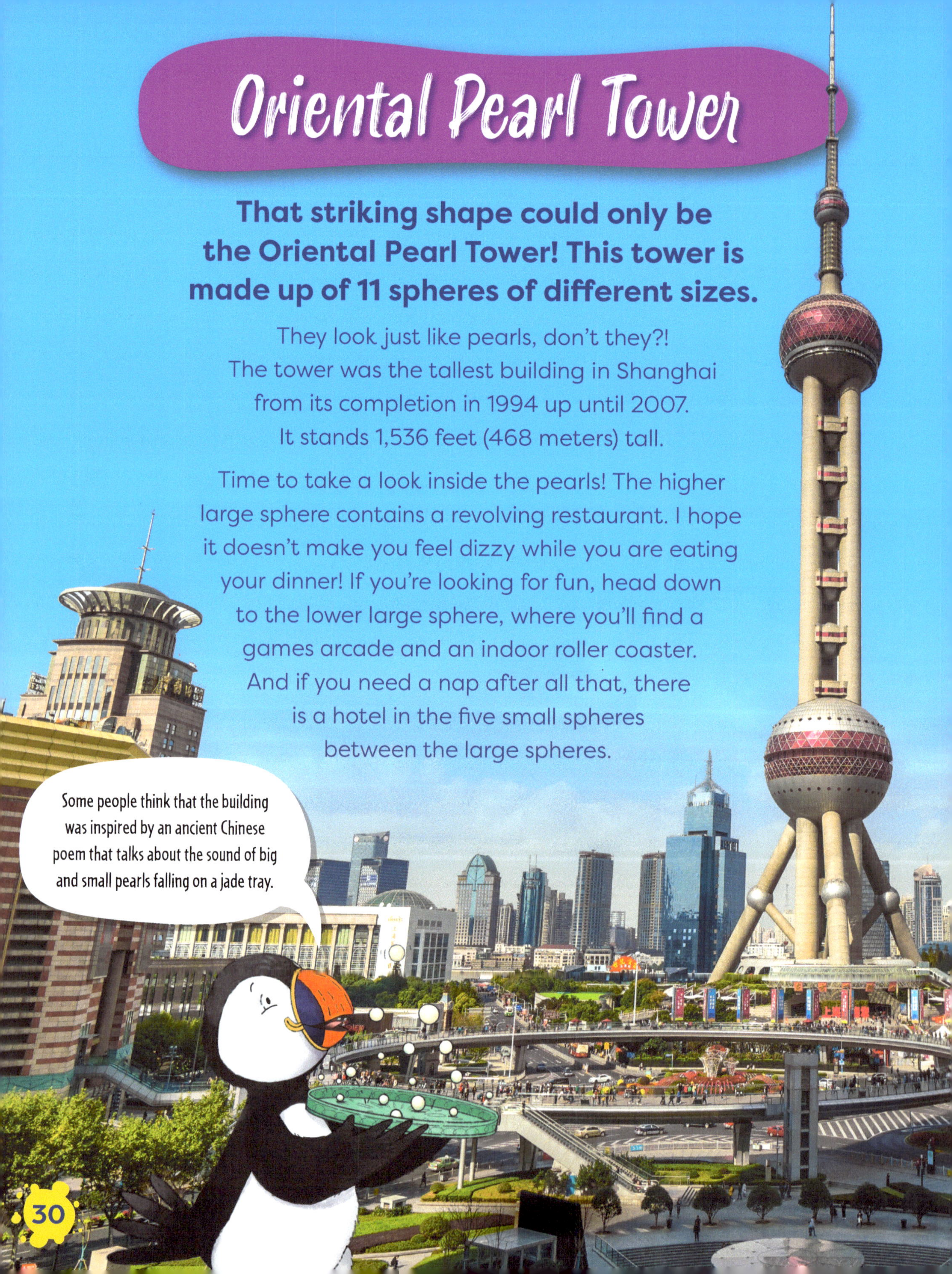

Oriental Pearl Tower

That striking shape could only be the Oriental Pearl Tower! This tower is made up of 11 spheres of different sizes.

They look just like pearls, don't they?! The tower was the tallest building in Shanghai from its completion in 1994 up until 2007. It stands 1,536 feet (468 meters) tall.

Time to take a look inside the pearls! The higher large sphere contains a revolving restaurant. I hope it doesn't make you feel dizzy while you are eating your dinner! If you're looking for fun, head down to the lower large sphere, where you'll find a games arcade and an indoor roller coaster. And if you need a nap after all that, there is a hotel in the five small spheres between the large spheres.

The Oriental Pearl Tower also serves a useful purpose. It's a TV tower, which helps to broadcast TV and radio programs across the city. The signals come from the tall antenna on top. Of the tower's overall height, 387 feet (118 meters) come from its antenna!

At night, LED lights on the outside of the Oriental Pearl Tower glow in the dark sky.

Century Park

Century Park is the largest park in Shanghai, so I've got to be in the right spot!

This massive park opened in the year 2000, which was the beginning of a new century. There's so much to do here ... I don't know where to begin!

I could play a game of mini golf, watch a show at the outdoor concert stage, or listen to relaxing bird songs in the bird reserve.

Oh, I know! My first stop has to be Mirror Lake. This is the largest artificial lake in Shanghai. The lake gets its name from its clear, calm water, which reflects the sky above like a mirror. Maybe I'll rent a boat and watch the clouds reflected in the water for a while.

If you visit Century Park in winter or spring, you'll be met with the beautiful sight and sweet smell of plum blossom. There are over 3,000 plum trees in the park. Many Shanghainese and tourists come every year to enjoy the experience.

There are fun surprises around every corner of Century Park, like these musicians made out of plants!

Shanghai Science and Technology Museum

If you want to learn more about robots, or just science and technology in general, head to Shanghai Science and Technology Museum!

This is one of China's most visited museums, so I know it's going to be really interesting. There are 14 different permanent exhibits, where you can learn about robots, space exploration, information technology, animals, and so much more!

You can see the glass "eggshell" from the outside of the building.

The robots exhibit shows robots doing fun things, such as playing the piano, shooting arrows, and painting pictures, as well as helpful tasks, such as cleaning the windows of tall skyscrapers.

There are also special galleries where you can learn more about Chinese inventions, explorers, and scientists. If you have time, check out one of the museum's IMAX theaters, where you can watch a 3-D movie. You wear special glasses that make it feel as if you could reach out and touch what's being shown on the screen!

Leave some time to explore the interesting design of the museum as well. It is laid out in a spiral shape, which rises up through the museum's five floors. This spiral represents scientific progress. The huge glass sphere in the center with a smaller sphere inside represent an egg and a yolk, which are symbols of new life in China.

China Art Museum

Inside this striking red building is the China Art Museum – a massive modern art museum.

It's filled with around 14,000 pieces of Chinese modern art. Unsurprisingly, it's one of the largest art museums in Asia! But this building wasn't always an art museum. It was built for the Expo 2010 world's fair, which was held in Shanghai. A world's fair is an international exposition that features exhibits dealing with commerce, industry, and science. Most fairs also offer entertainment and cultural activities and promote tourism in a region or country. Countries, charities, and private companies all build pavilions where they put on displays.

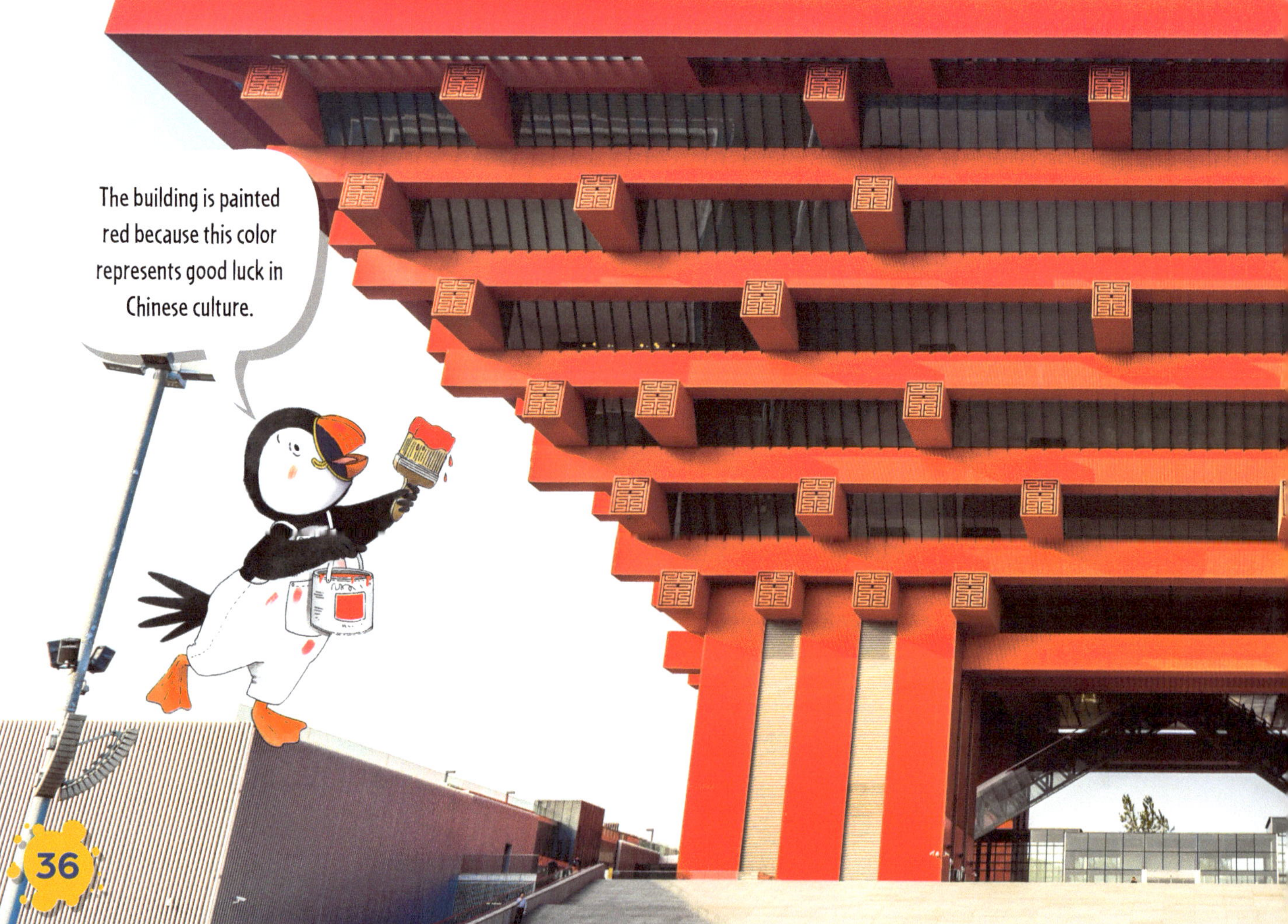

There were many pavilions and displays from other countries and organizations at the Shanghai Expo 2010. It was visited by 73 million people between May 1st and October 31st in 2010.

The design of the building was inspired by traditional Chinese roofs and ancient ding cauldrons, like the ones I saw earlier at the Shanghai Museum!

This building was the Chinese pavilion. It contained displays about how to develop cities and urban areas while still protecting the natural world. It was one of the largest displays ever seen at a world's fair! After Expo 2010, it was decided that the building would become the new home of the Shanghai Art Museum. It was renamed the China Art Museum.

These ears can only mean one thing!

Shanghai Disneyland Resort

Oh wow! There's a Disneyland right here in Shanghai!

Shanghai Disneyland Resort became the first Disneyland in mainland China when it opened in 2016. In addition to the main Disneyland theme park, the resort contains hotels, restaurants, stores, and parking for the resort's many guests.

Inside the Disneyland theme park are seven themed areas. Which area shall I visit first? Fantasyland with a princess theme? Pirate-themed Treasure Cove? Or futuristic Tomorrowland? I know ... the Gardens of Imagination! This area is the center of the park. It is filled with Chinese-style gardens. One of its gardens has mosaics in which the twelve animals of the Chinese zodiac are represented by different Disney characters!

The Enchanted Storybook Castle is found in the Fantasyland area of the park. It's the tallest castle ever built at a Disneyland, at 197 feet (60 meters) tall.

On this carousel, you can ride on the back of Dumbo the flying elephant from the Disney film *Dumbo*.

Each section of the park has different rides and roller coasters to enjoy. If you want something a bit calmer, why not watch a parade or stage show. Everywhere you look there are Disney characters to meet and greet. Oh look, there's my favorite character! I'm going to go say hi!

Zhujiajiao

Welcome to Zhujiajiao! This ancient town is located on the outskirts of Shanghai.

Some people call it the "Venice of Shanghai" because there are so many canals and rivers here! Just like Venice, the best way to get around Zhujiajiao is by boat. That must be what my oar is for!

As you'd expect in a canal town, there are also lots of bridges in Zhujiajiao - over 30 in fact! There are many different types and shapes of bridge, built from stone, marble, and wood. I wonder if I can cross all of them on my visit today?!

Between the rivers are narrow streets filled with interesting, historical buildings. In the past, these buildings were warehouses, banks, and rice stores. Today they are mostly restaurants and stores for the many tourists that visit this area. There are also many traditional Chinese homes. It must be fun waking up to a view of the river!

Fangsheng Bridge is one of the most important landmarks in Zhujiajiao. The Chinese word "fangsheng" means "freeing life." This meaning comes from a ceremony that monks used to hold on the bridge, in which they released live fish into the water.

Food

Trying new dishes in a city is always something to celebrate! I love tasting traditional foods, and I can't wait to see what Shanghai has to offer.

Get energized for a long day of sightseeing with a traditional Shanghainese breakfast. The four most popular breakfast items here are known as the "four warriors"!

There are sesame pancakes, fried dough, sticky rice rolls, and soy milk. Which would you like for your breakfast?

Some people like to soak their fried dough in hot soy milk before eating.

These dumplings, known as xiaolongbao, have a tasty secret inside – hot, delicious soup! To eat it properly, bite a small hole in the top of the dumpling, leave briefly to cool, slurp out the soup, and then eat the dumpling!

A Shanghainese chef told me the secret to getting the soup inside the dumpling. Do you want to know what it is? Well, when the soup is cool, it sets solid – a bit like Jell-O. This solid soup is placed inside the dumpling. When the dumpling is steamed, the soup melts back into a liquid. How clever!

If you visit in the autumn, you have to try Shanghai hairy crab. It's not hard to find ... they're on the menu everywhere – cafes, restaurants, and even vending machines! Steaming is the most traditional way of preparing a hairy crab. They are eaten with a simple sauce of ginger and vinegar. Yum!

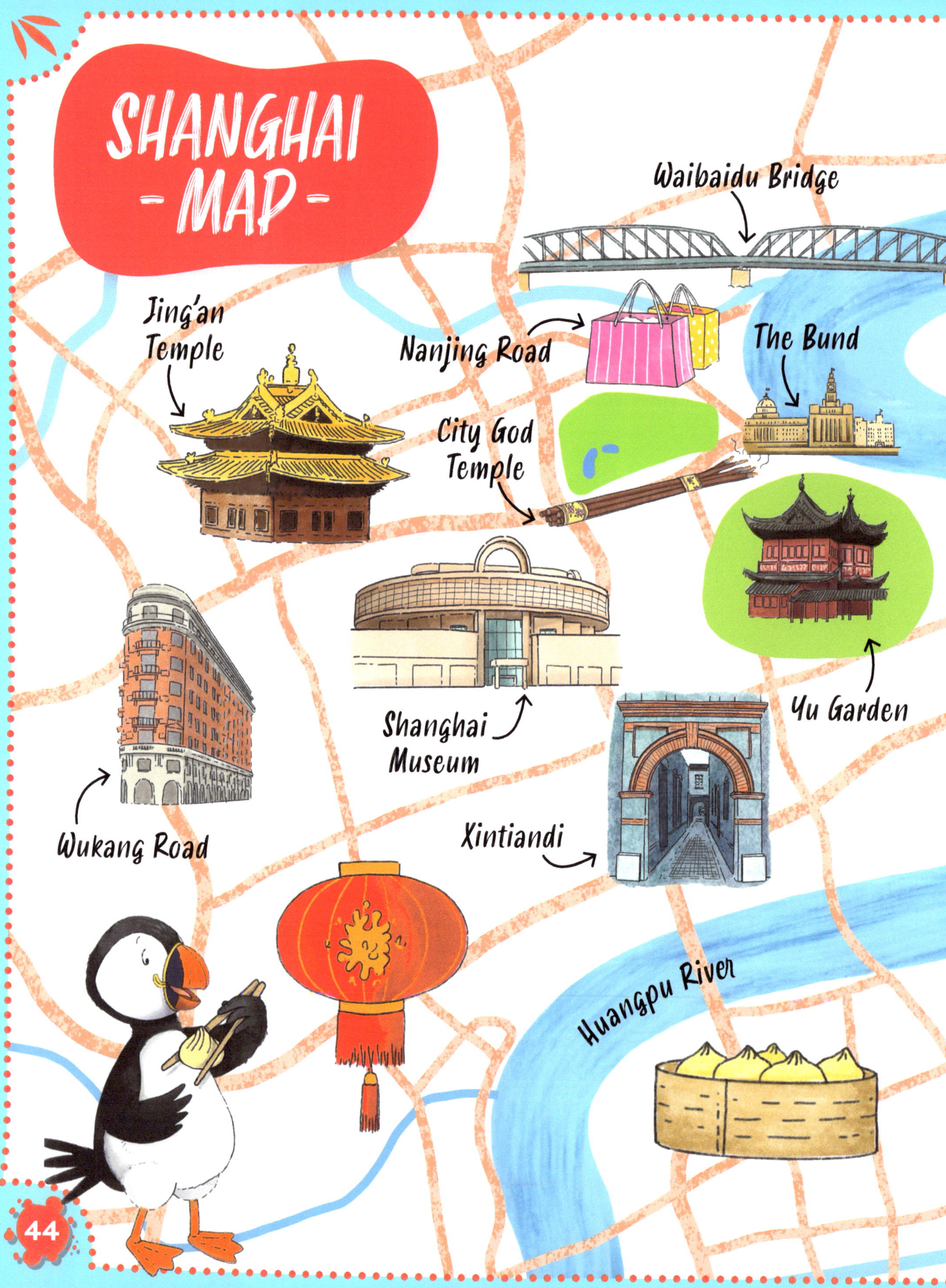
SHANGHAI
- MAP -
Waibaidu Bridge
Jing'an Temple
Nanjing Road
The Bund
City God Temple
Yu Garden
Shanghai Museum
Wukang Road
Xintiandi
Huangpu River

Oriental Pearl Tower
Shanghai Tower
Shanghai Science and Technology Museum
Century Park
Longyang Road station
China Art Museum

A Day in Shanghai

Zao shang hao! That means "good morning" in Mandarin Chinese, the official language of Shanghai.

Enjoy a morning stroll through Century Park. Keep your eyes to the sky and your ears perked! Many species of bird call this park home.

Did you spot any magpies in the trees?

Make your way over to Nanjing Road and shop for some Shanghai souvenirs. Be sure to try some traditional food for lunch!

Moon cakes can be sweet or savory. They are often filled with bean paste, lotus seeds, dried fruits and nuts, or other delicious ingredients.

Hop on the Shanghai Metro, the world's largest metro system by length, and travel to the China Art Museum. Here, you can view modern, contemporary, 21st-century, and historical Chinese art, as well as other special exhibitions.

It's time to take in another famous art form – architecture! Enjoy a riverboat cruise on the Huangpu River.

What iconic buildings along the Shanghai skyline do you recognize?

Finish your day in Shanghai with a bang – literally! – with the spectacular fireworks show at Shanghai Disneyland Resort.

It is believed the first fireworks were developed in China during the Han Dynasty.

Where Am I?

Destination 1

Prior to 1950, this location was home to a British racetrack.

You can visit many important buildings and museums located around this site.

This destination is the largest public open space in all Shanghai!

Destination 2

The spiral design of this building represents progress in its field of study.

Catch a 3-D movie at one of the IMAX theaters located here.

Learn about robots, information technology, animals, space exploration, and more at this destination.

Destination 3

An antenna on top of this building helps broadcast TV and radio programs across Shanghai.

From restaurants and hotels to a game arcade and even an indoor roller coaster, this destination is chock full of fun!

This iconic building includes 11 spheres of varying sizes.

Destination 4

This sacred destination is over 600 years old!

Markets, stores, and food stalls have popped up over the years, making this a busy destination for tourists and locals alike.

The main building at this destination is dedicated to three Chenghuang, gods who protect the city.

Destination 5

You're sure to spot this iconic building from the People's Square!

The shape of this building was inspired by a ding, an ancient Chinese pot with legs.

Visitors can enjoy over 12,000 pieces of ancient Chinese art here.

Destination 6

Many famous Chinese movie stars lived here in the 1930's and 1940's.

The architecture here includes French and British influence as well as Art Deco styles.

This destination was part of the French concession in Shanghai between 1849 and 1946.

Answers on page 55

Photos from Shanghai

Jing'an Temple

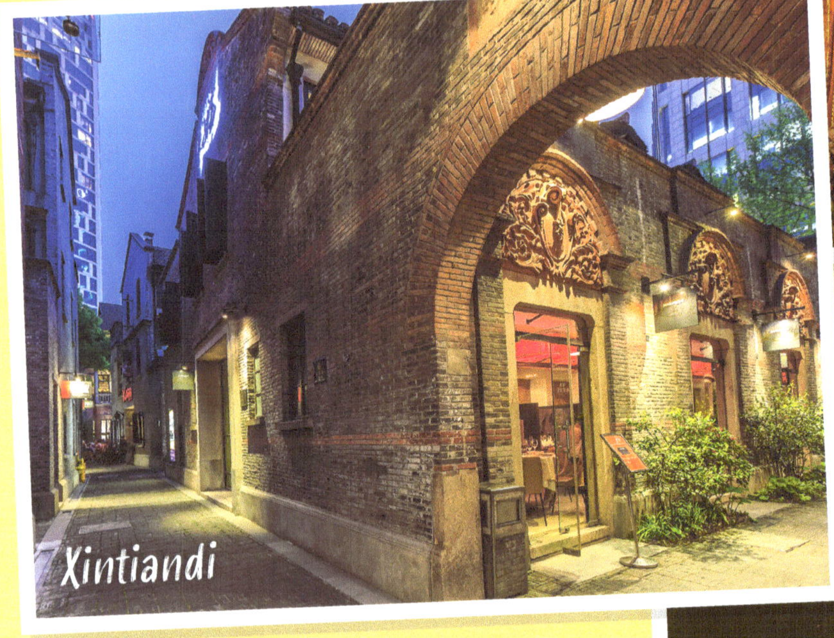
Xintiandi

Yu Garden

Zhujiajiao

The Bund

Shanghai Skyline

Waibaidu Bridge

Engage Your Reader

Activate background knowledge, set the purpose for reading, and monitor comprehension with this tried-and-true reading strategy!

Work with your reader(s) to create a KWL chart. Take some time to discuss what students already KNOW about Shanghai as well as what they WONDER about the city. You will revisit what they LEARNED after reading the book.

KNOW	WONDER	LEARNED

1. Have readers preview the structure of this text by flipping through the pages. Page 5 describes how clues are included for Norrie the puffin's next destinations.
2. Set the tone for reading: *As you read, think about all the different places in Shanghai and how history, culture, and people have shaped them into what they are today.*
3. After reading each section, revisit the KWL chart. Brainstorm what readers LEARNED from this section and add it to the chart. Your reader can add other wonderings they may have had, too!

Consider these questions to guide the brainstorming process:

- Why is location important to places, history, and culture?
- What patterns do you notice in the placement of things around the city of Shanghai?
- What makes Shanghai unique?

Use these comprehension questions to help your reader(s) check their understanding as they navigate the text.

p. 6-7 What are maglev trains and how do they work?

p. 8-9 What were concessions in Shanghai?

p. 10-11 Describe the shikumen houses found in today's Xintiandi shopping district.

p. 12-13 What five religions are recognized by the Chinese government?

Why are lion statues often placed outside of Chinese buildings?

p. 14-15 After stopping by People's Square, which nearby destination would you be most interested in visiting? Why?

p. 16-17 What does the shape of the Shanghai Museum represent?

p. 18-19 Describe the eastern and western stretches of the famous Nanjing Road.

p. 20-21 Why do many buildings on the Bund have traditional Western styles of architecture?

p. 22-23 Would you rather visit the Waibaidu Bridge or the Yangpu Bridge? Why?

p. 24-25 How old is City God Temple?

Why do people visit it today?

p. 26-27 The Yu Garden bridge that leads to the teahouse has nine turns. Why is this?

p. 28-29 What makes something a "megatall" building?

If you went to Shanghai Tower, what would you visit and why?

p. 30-31 Other than being a fun location to visit, what useful purpose does Oriental Pearl Tower serve?

p. 32-33 What would you enjoy most about a visit to Century Park? Why?

p. 34-35 What does the architecture of the Shanghai Science and Technology Museum represent?

p. 36-37 Today, the China Art Museum houses over 14,000 pieces of modern Chinese art, but what was this building's original purpose?

p. 38-39 What would you enjoy most about a visit to Shanghai Disneyland Resort?

p. 40-41 What makes Zhujiajiao a unique town on the outskirts of Shanghai?

p. 42-43 Which Shanghainese food are you most interested in trying? Why?

Extend Through Writing

Norrie the puffin just took you on a tour of Shanghai, China! Based on the places highlighted in this book, where would you like to visit in Shanghai?

Your written response should include:

- An introduction, including a general statement about Shanghai
- At least three places you would like to visit and at least three reasons why these places interest you
- A conclusion in which you briefly restate your interest in these three famous Shanghai destinations

Copy this graphic organizer onto another sheet of paper or visit **www.worldbook.com/resources** to download and print a copy. Use it to help you plan your writing.

<table>
<tr><td colspan="3">Introduction:</td></tr>
<tr><td>Destination 1</td><td>Destination 2</td><td>Destination 3</td></tr>
<tr><td>Reason 1</td><td>Reason 1</td><td>Reason 1</td></tr>
<tr><td>Reason 2</td><td>Reason 2</td><td>Reason 2</td></tr>
<tr><td>Reason 3</td><td>Reason 3</td><td>Reason 3</td></tr>
<tr><td colspan="3">Conclusion:</td></tr>
</table>

Answers

Where Am I? answers, p. 48-49:

1. People's Square, 2. Shanghai Science and Technology Museum, 3. Oriental Pearl Tower, 4. City God Temple, 5. Shanghai Museum, 6. Wukang Road

Comprehension question answers, p. 53:

p. 6-7

Maglev trains use magnetic force to float above the tracks. Because there is no friction between the train car and the track, they can travel quite quickly!

p. 8-9

In the past, certain neighborhoods in Shanghai were ruled over and settled by people from other countries. For example, Wukang Road was part of the French concession in China from 1849 to 1946.

p. 10-11

Shikumen houses were tall, brick townhouses that combined aspects of both Western and Chinese architecture. Today, many of these houses have been converted into stores, restaurants, and cafes.

p. 12-13

The Chinese government officially recognizes Buddhism, Taoism, Islam, Protestantism, and Catholicism as religions.

Lion statues are often placed outside Chinese buildings because these fierce animals are believed to be protectors.

p. 14-15

Answers may vary.

p. 16-17

The Shanghai Museum was designed to look like a ding, a type of ancient Chinese pot. In addition, the round top and square base reflect the ancient Chinese idea that the sky is round and Earth is square.

p. 18-19

Nanjing Road runs both east and west from People's Square. To the east, it is one of the busiest shopping streets in the entire world! To the west, visitors can enjoy historic hotels and luxury shopping centers.

p. 20-21

Many buildings on the Bund have traditional Western styles of architecture because many banks, trade centers, and custom houses were built by the people living in Shanghai's foreign concessions. The foreigners used architectural styles with which they were familiar.

p. 22-23

Answers may vary.

p. 24-25

City God Temple is over 600 years old!

Today, people visit the temple to worship the city gods and admire the beautiful decorations, statues, and architecture.

p. 26-27

The Yu Garden bridge that leads to the teahouse has nine turns because nine is considered a lucky number in China. It is said that crossing the bridge will bring you good luck!

p. 28-29

In order for something to be classified as a "megatall" building, it must reach at least 1,969 feet (600 meters) in height.

Answers may vary.

p. 30-31

In addition to being a fun location to visit, Oriental Pearl Tower serves a useful purpose as it helps broadcast TV and radio programs throughout Shanghai.

p. 32-33

Answers may vary.

p. 34-35

The spiral shape of the Shanghai Science and Technology Museum represents the scientific process. The glass sphere in the center of the building was designed to represent an egg and yolk, symbolizing new life.

p. 36-37

The China Art Museum building originally opened in 2010. It was created specifically for the Expo 2010 world's fair as the Chinese Pavilion and contained one of the largest exhibits ever seen at a world's fair.

p. 38-39

Answers may vary.

p. 40-41

Zhujiajiao is an ancient town located on the outskirts of Shanghai. The best way to travel around this unique town is by boat! There are over 30 bridges as well as plenty of stores, restaurants, and traditional Chinese homes here.

p. 42-43

Answers may vary.

Glossary

Buddhism *(BOO dihz uhm)* A religion started in India by a man named Siddhartha Gautama. His followers called him the *Buddha,* which means *Enlightened One.* An enlightened person is someone who is wise, fair, and thoughtful.

Chenghuang *(chuhng hwahng)* In Chinese folk religion, a god who protects a city and all the people who live in it

concession *(kuhn SEHSH uhn)* A special area for foreigners

ding *(dihng)* An ancient Chinese pot with legs

Shanghainese *(SHANG hy NEES)* A person who lives in the city of Shanghai

shikumen *(SHIH koo mehn)* A tall brick townhouse built around a narrow alleyway

Index

www.ingramcontent.com/pod-product-compliance
Ingram Content Group UK Ltd.
Pitfield, Milton Keynes, MK11 3LW, UK
UKHW060105300726
14090UKWH00003B/380
9780716653318